Patrick Mahomes
The Journey of a Football Hero

By Jon Hurst
with illustrations by
Cristian S. Aluas

Patrick Mahomes: The Journey of a Football Hero
Jon Hurst
With Illustrations by Cristian S. Aluas
Design by Penny Brucker

Paperback ISBN: 979-8-9887170-1-0

Once upon a time, there was a boy named Patrick Mahomes who loved playing football.

He grew up to be a famous quarterback in the NFL (National Football League). The quarterback is the player who throws the ball to their teammates.

Patrick has won a lot of championship games and been named the MVP (Most Valuable Player) in the league two times.

He will be remembered as one of the greatest quarterbacks ever.

Before Patrick became famous, he was just a regular kid. He was born on September 17, 1995 in Tyler, Texas. His dad played Major League Baseball.

Growing up, Patrick's favorite food was ketchup. He put it on eggs, macaroni and cheese, and everything else. He even used to eat ketchup sandwiches!

In school, Patrick loved playing football, baseball, and basketball.

2013-2014

MALE ATHLETE OF THE YEAR

He was so good at all three sports that he won an award for being the best athlete.

When Patrick was still in high school, he was asked to play for a professional baseball team called the Detroit Tigers. He went to college instead.

Patrick knew he would have to choose between football and baseball. He picked football because he loved it the most.

In 2017, Patrick entered the NFL Draft. That's when the pro football teams pick new players. Lots of coaches came to watch him practice. His passes were as fast as race cars!

On draft day, the Kansas City Chiefs picked Patrick. They were so excited to have him on their team.

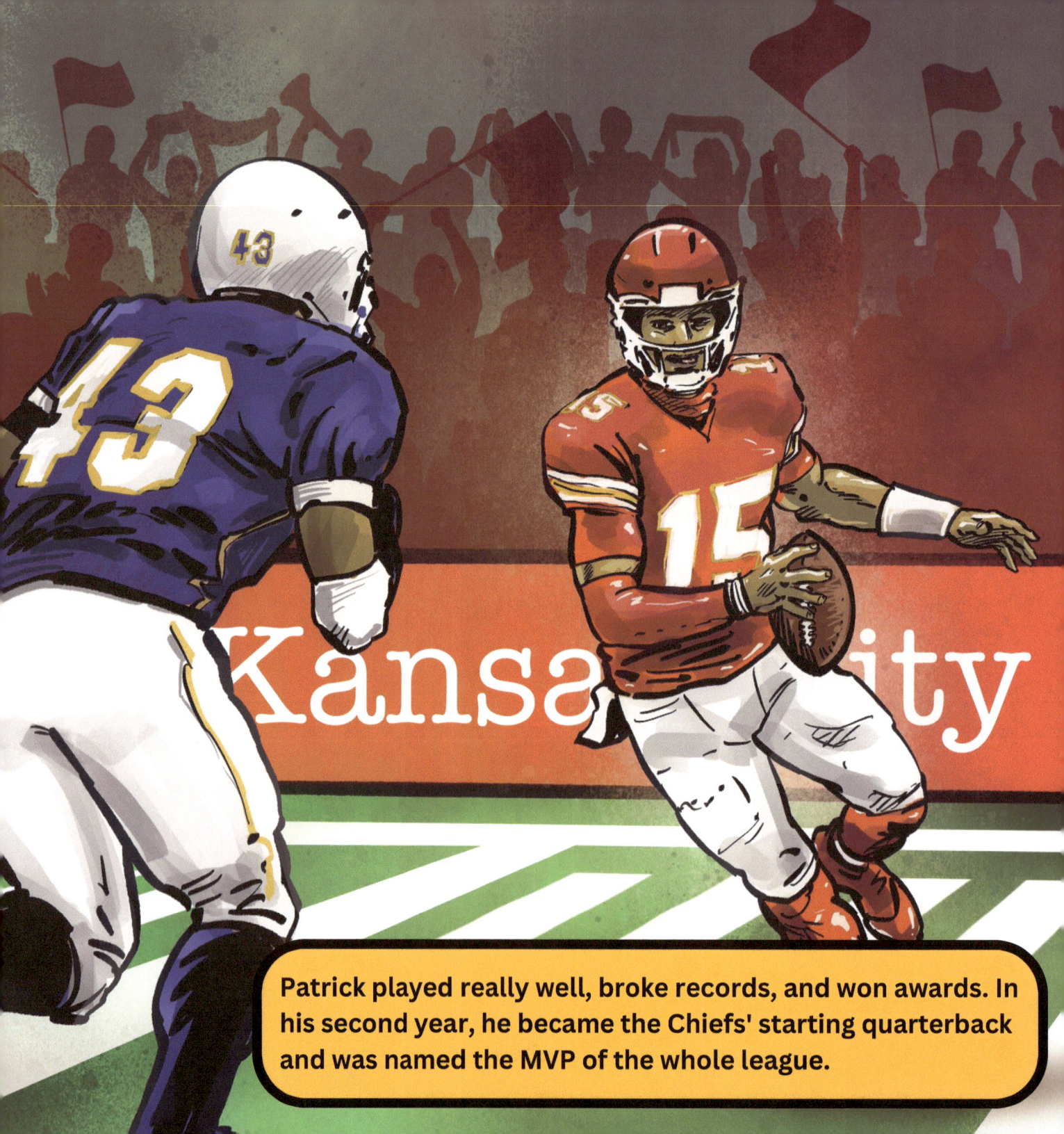

Patrick played really well, broke records, and won awards. In his second year, he became the Chiefs' starting quarterback and was named the MVP of the whole league.

In his third season, Patrick led the Chiefs to the Super Bowl and won! Patrick was named the Super Bowl's MVP -- the youngest person ever to earn the award.

In 2023, Patrick and the Chiefs played the Philadelphia Eagles in the Super Bowl.

Even though Patrick had hurt his ankle, he played an incredible game, and the Chiefs won the Super Bowl once more!

Patrick isn't just about football. He is known for his kindness and started a charity to help kids.

Off the field, Patrick found love and marriage with his high school sweetheart, Brittany. They live in Kansas City, Missouri, and have two beautiful children.

He plays the game in a unique and creative way, making mind-blowing passes and leading his team to victory.

Patrick Mahomes is more than just a football player; he is a legend. His story shows us that with hard work, determination, and a little bit of magic, we can achieve our dreams, just like Patrick did.

www.ingramcontent.com/pod-product-compliance
Lightning Source LLC
Chambersburg PA
CBHW041611120626
46551CB00002B/406